sharing

AUNTY FAY MUIR & SUE LAWSON

ILLUSTRATED BY

LEANNE MULGO WATSON

When we share,
there is plenty for all.
Take, use what you need.

Water for drinking,
washing,
cleansing spirits.

Fire for cooking, warmth
and caring for Country.

Branches for tools,
shelter,
resting places.

Tall grass for nets, baskets
and binding tools.

Ochre for ceremony,

for stories and art.

Seeds and roots
for eating and healing.

Take only what you need,
no more, no less.

Give back
what you can.

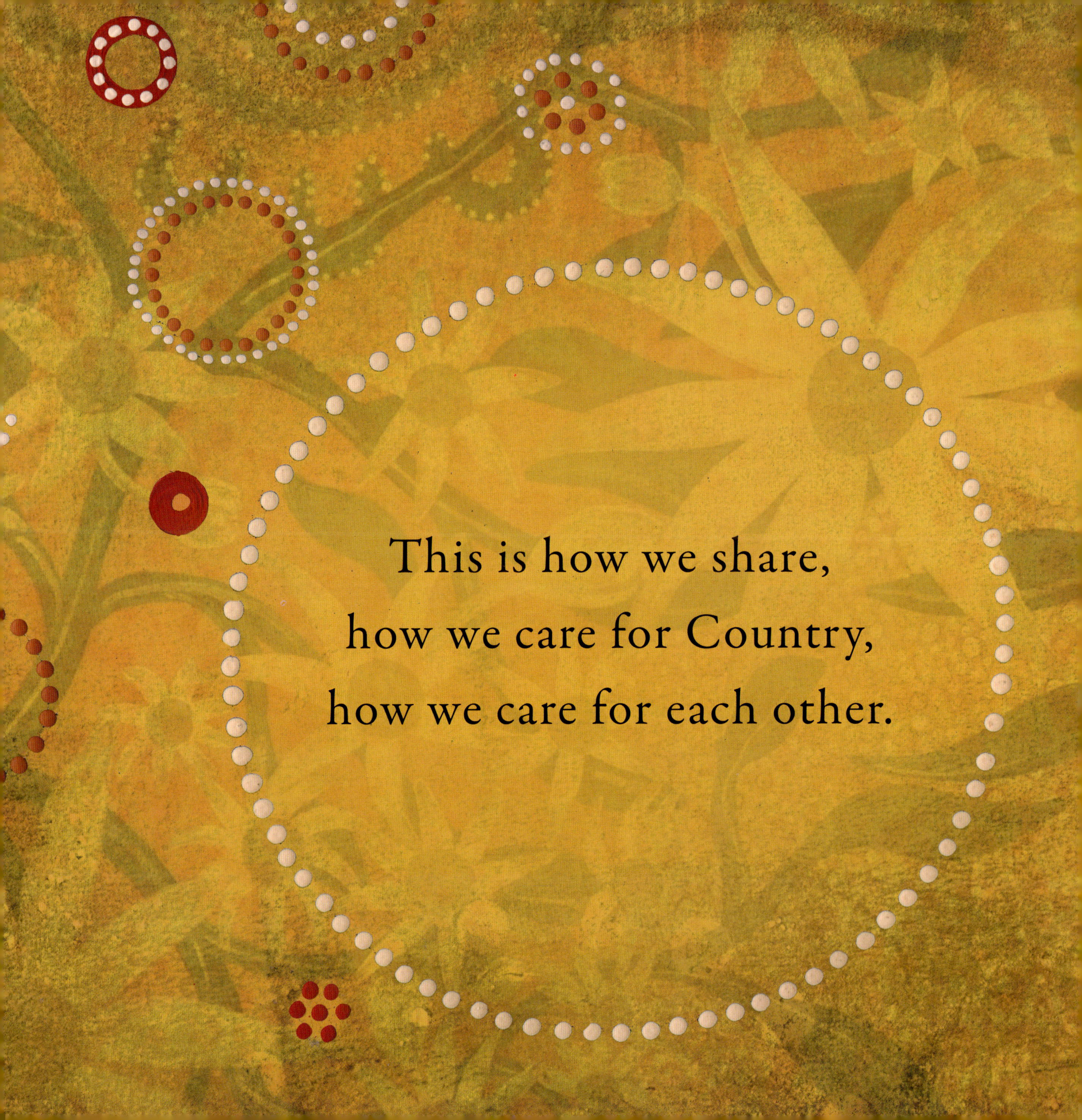

This is how we share,
how we care for Country,
how we care for each other.

This is a Magabala Book

Leading Publisher of Aboriginal and Torres Strait Islander Storytellers.

Changing the World, One Story at a Time.

First published 2021. Reprinted 2022, 2023, 2025 x 2
Magabala Books Aboriginal Corporation
1 Bagot Street, Broome, Western Australia
Website: www.magabala.com Email: sales@magabala.com

Magabala Books is assisted by the Australian Government through Creative Australia, its principal arts investment and advisory body, and publishes with support from the WA Government.

Magabala Books is Australia's leading independent Aboriginal and Torres Strait Islander publishing house. We acknowledge the Traditional Owners of the Country on which we live and work. We recognise the unbroken connection to traditional lands, waters and cultures. Through what we publish, we honour all our Elders, peoples and stories, past, present and future.

Printed in China by Toppan Leefung

The illustrations in this book were created with mixed media, including acrylic paint, geli-prints, torn painted paper and digital collage.

ISBN 978-1-925768-74-9

Packaged by Ballantyne Rawlins in collaboration with Magabala Books.

OUR PLACE logo is made from original art by Lisa Kennedy.

A catalogue record for this book is available from the National Library of Australia

For my brother, R.G.S. – one with nature and the bush. F.S-M.

For Katie, my sister and my friend. S.L.

For my mudjin – family.
You are my budbud – heart. L.M.W.

Fay is a Boonwurrung Elder who cares about sharing her First Nation culture and stories with all children to enjoy and take on a journey of learning.

Sue's award-winning young adult and children's books are recognised for the sensitive way they explore the exciting and heartbreaking complexities of growing up. Her first book with Aunty Fay was *Nganga: Aboriginal and Torres Strait Islander Words and Phrases*.

Leanne is a Darug woman from the Booroborongal people of the Dyirabun – Hawkesbury region of New South Wales. Her previous Magabala book, *Cooee Mittigar – A Story on Darug Songlines*, with Jasmine Seymour, won the 2020 Prime Minister's Award for Literature in the Children's Literature category.

The creators wish to acknowledge that Sharing was written on Wadawurrung, and illustrated on Darug people's lands.

The creators wish to acknowledge that Sharing was written on Wadawurrung, and illustrated on Darug people's lands.